Four and Twenty Blackbirds

Margot Hover

LOS ANGELES † NEW YORK † LONDON † MELBOURNE

Four and Twenty Blackbirds by Margot Hover

978-1-947240-72-8   Paperback

978-1-947240-73-5   eBook

Copyright © 2023 Margot Hover. All rights reserved.

First Printing 2023

Cover art by Dennis Callaci

Layout and design by Mark Givens

For information:

Bamboo Dart Press

chapbooks@bamboodartpress.com

Bamboo Dart Press 034

www.pelekinesis.com

www.bamboodartpress.com

www.shrimperrecords.com

CONTENTS

Introduction 5

Why I Write 9

The Honey Girl Saga: chapter 1 12

What do I think about change? 15

Secondhand 19

Me, too? 23

Once a Catholic, always…? 26

"This place is not long for the world." – Christian hymn 29

My places 32

Lose a Place; Find a Place 37

Prends Courage! 40

If I could just listen… 43

Heirloom 47

Transcendence vs fear/folly 50

About the Author 55

INTRODUCTION

When Covid struck nearly three years ago, my heart ached for the thousands of victims who died by themselves, as well as for their families and the staffs who were caught in such vastly unthinkable and hereto for unimaginable situations. But, living in an (overly) busy retirement community, I confess that I was glad when our pace necessarily slowed to a crawl. Our community lunchtime, usually a daily leisurely coming together, was reduced to masked six-foot-apart lines to pick up plastic boxes of food. That added nearly two hours of found time to my day. Zoomed meetings eliminated travel time. Leisure activities—movies, concerts, and restaurant dinners with friends—vanished altogether. Extroverts among us languished, while introverts caught our breath and were quietly grateful for the respite.

I am an introvert. I relished the hours of uninterrupted time to indulge whims and dreams I had no time to develop and enjoy before. I joined a contemplative prayer group that zoomed together every late afternoon, providing a thoughtful, restful transition from daytime projects to quieter evenings. I was invited to submit an article to an online newsletter which led to an invitation to join a weekly writers' group. I enjoy writing, and authoring books and articles has always been part of my work. But this was a chance to explore more personal themes and to learn from writers with a similar agenda, from widely differing backgrounds.

And finally, I created a blog. I have no idea where that inspiration came from. But a good friend and neighbor of mine one day shared what she thought should be my epitaph: Maggie possesses a wry sense of doom. With that, I was off and running with my new best friends, Blue Host and Word Press. After a month of anxious days before my computer and sleepless nights populated by images of evil hackers, I produced "apocketfullofwry.com." Some of those entries have found their way into this book.

The writers' group was the brainchild of Daniel Pryfogle, Executive Director of a nonprofit, Sympara, a service that provides consultation to churches seeking to repurpose assets and buildings they no longer need. It seemed to Daniel that elders themselves have talents that can be repurposed for the common good, and so the model of writing groups was born. Our group has been remarkably consistent in membership, and as remarkable in variety. For nearly 3 years, we have met weekly for six one-hour sessions with Daniel as our participant – facilitator. At the end of each hour, Daniel suggests the topic for our writing for the next week, to be emailed to all the day before our group meeting. Our group has agreed to continue to meet and write without him during the six – to – eight week interim between units. Some of my essays for that group have been included in this collection.

For Myers-Briggs aficionados, I am an intuitive, feeling, introverted, perceiver. While those gifts were tailor-made for my work as a clinical pastoral educator in congregational and medical settings, I think they have also provided a good foundation now for my love of writing more personally. For example, where outlining was useful when I was writing research articles and reports for journals in my professional field, now I love writing as a way of uncovering and discovering what I think and feel about a topic. I love storytelling and watching stories unfold around me. I love the taste and texture of fine words. I learned to read with my mother's copies of the *New Yorker*. In the first grade, I was the only five-year-old who could use—and spell—"unique" and "panache." I indulged all of that in my blog and with my writers' group.

In another stroke of magnificent coincidence and heavenly blessing, Joy Alvarez, Director of the Upland Public Library Adult Literacy Program, introduced me to several colleagues and friends, among them Dennis and Allen Callaci. Musicians, performers, writers, editors and publishers—they are remarkably gifted, creative, and generous. They introduced me to other writers who have become friends, and it was Dennis's idea to publish a collection of my work. I am profoundly grateful.

So there you have it! These three years have brought a richness I never could have imagined. I am profoundly grateful for every bit of it. I do confess to a twinge of guilt every once in a while. My "retirement" home, Pilgrim Place, is a community of elders all of whom have spent—and still spend—our lives working for social justice and care of the environment. Despite my continuing commitment to those efforts, I sometimes wonder if it is self-indulgent to devote my time and thought to exploring the meaning of elderhood, of aging, for me, for my soul, for what remains of my life here. My conscience is helped in that consideration by the fact that my feet hurt, I see more doctors now than I did in the preceding 80 years of my life, and sitting still at my typewriter is uncommonly attractive.

So let's see if it has been a waste of time, shall we.

WHY I WRITE

Many years ago, as the story has it, someone asked an Inuit folk artist about his approach. He replied, "I carve the stone until I discover what is hiding there for me to find." I write pretty much the same way. Something strikes me, but I don't yet know why. I hold it in my soul, turn it over and around, carry it with me as I move through my day. Then, when it's time, I begin to write, and as I do, the story's meaning emerges piece by piece, layer by layer. By the time I finish, I begin to see why the story spoke to me. Like the Inuit artist, I learn what is hiding in the initial experience, waiting for me to discover it.

The time of my writing about theory and practice in my profession has probably waned. For many years, I wrote about education for ministry and research in that field. Earlier, my work focused on religious awareness and practice in the fabric of daily family life as it is really lived. My theory was that everything is holy in some way. Absolutely everything! I wrote table graces around spilled milk, benedictions around family fracases, dedications of new school shoes and bookbags, blessings of firsts and lasts. This is what I learned, the shape that emerged when I shared my words: very few readers used my rituals and liturgies as they appeared. What I heard most often was, "We didn't use your suggestions, but they helped us to recognize and claim the importance and holiness of the rituals we already practice." My ideas, born of the messiness of my days, freed readers to acknowledge their own messy births and deaths, learnings and losses, regrets and reconciliations, their own sacred lives.

As a writer and teacher, then, my discovery was both blessing and curse. I couldn't get by with easy answers or rosy pictures. I remember taking my elderly mother with me when I taught a course in parenting as part of a parish adult education program. One mother asked how to deal with her four-year-old's volcanic temper tantrums. I was delivering a long dissertation on strategic interventions when my mother, rolling her eyes, interrupted from the back of the room: "You do know, she's a four-year-old, after all." Once again, I learned that I had to be authentic.

Now I'm old. I still love the sound of good words carefully carved. Now I have the time and the taste for the writing I did in my journal many years ago. I still have something to say. The niche where I spent much of my professional life was the clinical formation of clergy and chaplains. I am shy now when the community organizers, seminary professors and missionaries in my retirement community speak about areas where I feel ignorant. While I have marched in my share of picket lines, I don't begin to know the history of the labor movement in Los Angeles. I religiously sort cans and bottles but still can't keep track of environmental legislation. I think of that old Sam Cooke song, "Don't know much about geography…"

So I write about the things I'm sure of, the aches and pains of my aging human heart, and the satisfaction and challenges of being old. Today, I took advantage of our Covid sequestration to clean closets. I boxed up the crochet books I bought whenever I felt flush for the day in my retirement when I would have time for handwork. Now I have the time but cannot hold a crochet hook. So as I wrapped the package to send to a younger, more able friend, I felt an ounce of regret but a pound of satisfaction at having completed one more piece of the process of letting go. Last year, I drove across the country to hand on to a much younger bandmate my beloved set of custom-made bagpipes which I had proudly played for 25 years. It was time

There is redemption in my story about that moment when it provides a connection with the heart of my congregation in the nursing home or assisted living facility. They listen and remember their own similar experiences with more acceptance, understanding that they are not alone. Like Jacob, in those moments of mutual recognition, we say, "Truly the Lord is in this place, although we did not know it." (Genesis 28.16) We are not alone.

June, 2022

THE HONEY GIRL SAGA: CHAPTER 1

God was certainly smiling on me when, in the last minutes of my four-day search for a place to live in Manhattan, New York, I found an apartment on East 83rd St. I should have known that the site was—how shall I put it—unusual—when I ventured out that first day to forage for supper for my son and myself. In the middle of a busy intersection, an elderly woman in a wheelchair snagged my sleeve. She pulled my head down to her level. "I hear you pray," she said. "Well, I've been known to do that," I replied. How did she know anything at all about me? I'd only been in town for three hours. "Pray for me," she ordered. "I have a touch of bone cancer." So there, with cars whizzing around us in the middle of the intersection at Second Avenue, I prayed for Nana, the 93-year-old grandma of East 83rd St.

That was only the beginning. Honey Girl, the matriarch of the block, took one look at my belongings, which filled my apartment and the hallway, and trailed down the steps onto the street outside. "You gotta do something with all that," she yelled. "You'll get robbed blind!" At that point, I was hoping I would be robbed since I had no idea how everything would fit in that apartment.

But it was August; I had driven my son from North Carolina that day, had picked up head lice from the movers, and now hoped to drown myself in the shower. I had just gotten nicely soaped up when the intercom screeched: "Get out here right now! Call 911! Somebody's stealing your car.

I should be so lucky, I thought, since I had no place to park and, I discovered, no need for a car anyway. But I knew if I didn't mount a token resistance, I would have Honey Girl to deal with. I threw on a shirt and ambled down the front steps. By that time, Honey Girl had beaten up the robber, who fled down the street.

At the same time a cruiser pulled up from the other direction. "Already took care of it," Honey Girl reported to the two very green cops in the front seat. "And I want this street closed off at both ends by eight o'clock tomorrow morning for our block party," she continued. "Sure," the two youngsters scoffed. Honey Girl hoisted her short but formidable frame through the cruiser window and grabbed both cops by the collars. "Listen to me! Now! I'm the mother of two New York City cops, and I want those barricades up at both ends by eight o'clock. Do you understand!" "Yes, ma'am," they whispered. And by eight o'clock the following day, the barricades were in place.

The following day, I encountered more of my neighbors. Honey Girl was the undisputed matriarch. She had lived with her husband, Bob, on the block for 40 years. She spent 23 hours of every day on the stoop at the center of the block of five-story brownstone walk-ups, just around the corner from Gracie mansion, Gloria Vanderbilt's high rise, and the East River promenade. Honey Girl declared coyly that she saved the remaining hour of each day for her husband.

Honey Girl was, shall we say, stocky. Bob worked the night shift underground repairing subway rails. When her boys were very young, Bob had a massive heart attack. Honey Girl had diabetes, but she prayed that if God let her husband live, she would give up insulin. Bob lived, and inexplicably, so did Honey Girl.

Big Bob and Big Mary worked as caregivers in city programs to help the elderly stay in their apartments. For many years, they sat on the stoop next door every evening, each tuned in to separate transistor radios where they listened to whatever ballgames were broadcast. When it snowed, they sat on the stairs just inside. One year, Honey Girl decided they should get married, and she ordered Big Bob to get an engagement ring for Christmas. When Christmas came and no ring appeared, Honey Girl produced a ring and proposed for him. Perhaps they are still sitting on the stoop, still with separate radios.

Nana lived on the fifth floor and so used my bathroom since she spent most of her days in her wheelchair on her stoop. More about her, TighterThanaGnat'sAssRoy, Crazy Louise, and the rest of the neighbors next time.

September 1995

WHAT DO I THINK ABOUT CHANGE?

As an introverted intuitive feeling perceiver (INFP) I almost never <u>think</u> about anything first; I feel my way into events that befall me until my thinking gets into gear. "Befall": that verb tells you how and what I think about change. The image that goes along with "change" for me is the elephant in the flouncy skirt leaping off the high dive into a bucket of water. But baby needs shoes, as the saying goes, so my head pushes me from behind and helps me recall all the times I've jumped and survived to tell the story.

I spent my professional life in institutions that changed suddenly without much regard for the people at the bottom. The new pastor closes the school, the Catholic hospital becomes a "for-profit," a new Pharaoh comes to town. Further, I developed a reputation as the "Mikey" of my profession. Someone would get a dab of money and the germ of an idea but would lack the will or stamina to put it together. Fortunately, the pharaohs and the opportunities often arrived simultaneously, thank God. My family never went hungry, and I gradually learned to live with my anxiety about diving.

But tonight, I was listening to my favorite podcast, Bitter Southerner ("Believing in a Different South"), as I did the dishes after supper. The guests were Congressman John Lewis and a young journalist; Together they created three award-winning graphic novels about Lewis's part in the civil rights movement. Although…. Although he has been fiery when situations demanded it, tonight, Congressman Lewis used his front porch voice to reflect on how his life took the shape it did. He was studying for the ministry when he read Martin Luther King's "Letter from Birmingham Jail," in which King muses sadly that the most significant obstacle in the struggle was the complacent inaction of clergy and other church leaders. The young journalist related reading his deceased father's sermons from that era, noticing the truth of King's observation.

I swallowed hard. Roman Catholic (therefore not ordained) woman as I am, those are my people. And this was the weekend of a national perfect storm. I put down my dishtowel, dried my hands, and went to my computer to Google King's letter. Before I could read it, a friend sent me Ta-Nehisi Coates' article, "The First White President." (*The Atlantic*, October 2021). Before I closed my computer, I received a Netflix note: "Based on your viewing history, we thought you would enjoy… "The first Black Man in San Francisco." Then I watched several hours of the Los Angeles riots.

Then, this morning, I found a notebook slipped under my door by a good friend struggling with her husband's descent into Alzheimer's. She, too, has been watching the news. Both of us are adopted parents of children of color. Her Black son died of a drug overdose; they left retirement to rear his infant daughter. My dark-skinned Cambodian son still blames me for placing him in psychiatric hospitals and group homes where the primary population happened to be African-American. I foster parented a 14-year-old dark-skinned Caucasian girl, pregnant with a Black boy; her parents were afraid that one or both of them would be lynched in their hometown. I know well the talk," and the futility of trying to prepare my children for danger and discrimination.

Given all that, here is what I think about change. I despair of true change ever happening in this country, and I am heartsick that the dreams and hopes of generations continue to be so far out of reach. From the beginning, America was built on the bodies of the conquered, and we seem to have no awareness of the depth of rage we've created and no sustained concrete will to deal with it except by subjugation.

While I was teaching at Duke, a young boy, who had for all intents and purposes been reared by kindly security officers on campus where he hung around, was convicted for the third time of some relatively minor crime. But in a "three strikes" state, he faced a life sentence in prison and was immediately transported across the state. On the way, he managed to overpower the driver of the police cruiser, stole his gun, and headed back to the only home he knew, at Duke campus. He occupied the chaplaincy offices for several hours before a police sharpshooter shot across the parking lot and street, through a window and down the hallway, striking the young man in the head. I stood with the boy's family in the ER as the blood-soaked gurney arrived. I can still hear their screams and feel their loss.

Now, tonight, I have so little patience for book groups and polite study projects. I wish Rodeo Drive had burned to the ground. What right do the rich have to a Whole Foods market when whole blocks in Los Angeles are designated "food deserts"? What right does the CEO of a health care corporation have to a salary that would have kept a failing Mississippi hospital for Black patients going for another three months?

What I know about change is that it always threatens the status quo, whether the subject is an internal change of my heart or change in a society where I have failed. And so tonight, I wearily don my tutu and head once more to the high dive.

December, 2021

SECONDHAND

One Christmas, many years ago, my adopted Cambodian daughter surprised me with a gift of a jacket. The coat was perfect: my size, washable, with pockets, a color that would go with everything, and a collar that came up around my ears when it was particularly chilly. And it was from my daughter, so that I felt wrapped in her love every time I wore it. But over the years, it shrank a little, and I expanded a little, so that my wrists hung out and the buttons never clasped as well as they did at first. After several months of thought, I reluctantly but lovingly turned it over to the community thrift shop. Several days later, I was filled with joy when I saw a friend ahead of me wearing The Coat. I was so happy that someone I loved so much now wore the gift from my daughter, whom I love so much. I could hardly contain my pleasure, and the next time I saw my friend, I told her the history of the coat she was now wearing. She seemed as pleased as I was.

But given a long time to reflect on the whole incident, I've come to think of it in a larger context. Most of us have in our homes at least one or two pieces that are special to us because of their history in our family, occupation or friendship circles. In even the smallest of our apartments one may find a picture of parents, a serving bowl that has been passed down through several generations, a potato masher that grandma used, or a piece of needlework a sister created to hang on the wall. A running joke here is the rapid turnover of clothing through the local Goodwill store, but I don't think we give due reverence to the recycling of all manner of clothing and miscellaneous, shoes and furniture, books and linens here in our little town.

A few months ago, an obviously well-cared-for rice bowl found its way there, and because I knew it had belonged to someone whose friendship I treasured, I snapped it up. It was too large for a single person and should not have been kept and not used, so after several months, I carefully wrapped it and sent it to my daughter. I called her before it was delivered and explained that I hoped she would treat it with care, fully expecting that it would have a hard life in her busy household. But not so! "Of course, I know what it is," she exclaimed. "I haven't seen a rice bowl like that since I was a child in Cambodia, where the monks used bowls to beg for their dinner. I shall love it!" Found Treasures!

Hand-me-downs! So many of the physical issues I deal with are genetic in origin; I wryly wonder if my sisters got "the good stuff." But the other day, I looked at my hands as I did some needlework. It startled me at how much like my mother's hands they appeared. At times in my life, I thought I was born to care for my parents. They were both needy, which probably accounts for my determination to be independent and self-reliant, come hell or high water.

But there were my hands, which have brought me such joy in my life. Without intending to, necessarily, I've undertaken to learn most of the arts and crafts my mother practiced throughout her life—knitting and crocheting, smocking, brush painting, printmaking and more. I drew the line at the piano, and took up bagpiping instead. But where for so long I struggled against her definition of me, now I remember with ease and pleasure the gifts she gave me. I don't know what my life would be like without her appreciation for beauty, nature and relationships, even and sometimes especially, difficult ones that, at the end of the day, embody love.

And then, I've been thinking about the rituals, prayers and practices I inherited from my church and my family. Those are the bones of my spirituality, regardless of the new theological "clothing" I have donned through the years. During Advent, I looked around for some practice that would help me reflect on the holiness of the season. It's the season for focusing on the role of Mary in the Gospels, and I decided to say the joyful mysteries of the rosary each day. I had just rediscovered my mother's rosary in the bottom of a jewelry box. It is remarkable to me how centering that practice still is as I pray for Mary's protection for today's refugees, families, and pharaohs. I notice something similar when we sing old familiar hymns; there's a happy sigh of recognition as the piano begins tunes we've heard all our lives.

I wonder about the other treasures, both material and spiritual, that I've received. There are the things I do for fun, for example—the creation of music, play, and handwork. How many of those have I inherited? I reflect on them, and honor those who have blessed me with them. All of that is "secondhand," and precious beyond accounting.

So now, I savor my "secondhand" memories as I slip my arms into the shawls and jackets of my history. I wrap them around my shoulders when my elder days are chilly. I smile at their peculiarities but embrace them as gifts, just as they are.

March, 2016

ME, TOO?

I live in a multi-faith retirement community where one requirement for entrance has always been that one has made a significant longtime commitment to peace, justice, and/or the environment. We have sometimes been referred to as "the conscience" of our town, since all of us continue to work hard and creatively toward a better world for all. And we do work hard.

So right now, with the George Floyd killing, the issue of racial injustice and police violence is on our front burner, and if we weren't already confined to our homes by Covid-19, our evening walks—with masks—were curtailed by a countywide 5 p.m. to 6 a.m. curfew. We think of little other than the mob violence that has tarnished the peaceful demonstrations not far away. When we aren't watching local TV stations or NPR for news, we are discussing those issues on our community Google group. Nearly everyone chimes in with their personal story. "I was on the march across the bridge," writes one resident. "My arm was broken by the local police during the Chicago riots, "writes another. "I tutored black middle schoolers for years," writes another. "My church ran an active social service center for the homeless," says another.

I have my stories, too, I think to myself. I tick off on my fingers the Cambodian war survivors, the black Amerasian, the troubled white teenagers whom I foster-parented or adopted. I know what it's like to give my beautiful brown-skinned son "The Talk." I remember my terror when we were separated on a crowded New York City bus, seeing a deranged homeless white gentleman verbally assault him. I knew that if the police were called, my son would end up at Riker's Island for years before being charged.

But something doesn't feel quite right about my impulse to share those stories. I think back on my many years as a hospital teaching chaplain. While it might've been helpful to tell a neighbor or good friend, "I know how you feel," that statement could demolish a pastoral relationship. The best thing I could do as a chaplain was to listen and to keep my mouth shut. If I absolutely could not tolerate that tension, I would say, "I am sorry. I am so, so sorry."

So now I wonder why we are so eager to tell <u>our</u> stories to those who have been beaten down for generations by violence and injustice. It feels like a grown-up version of the childhood claim, "Not me, mom. That was really bad, but <u>I</u> didn't do it." As a formerly Catholic laywoman, systemic injustice is always before me, but I have never been denied a home that I could otherwise afford, in a neighborhood I liked. I have never been followed by a security officer while shopping. I have never been pulled out of my car and arrested for driving with a faulty headlight. I have never had a teacher call me "stupid" or refuse to help me with a lesson I found difficult. I've never spent years in solitary confinement. None of my schoolmates were ever shot to death.

It may be that the fairly recent recognition of white privilege might change the dialogue. With 200 years of being on top, I'm pretty pessimistic. Nevertheless, I found myself on the verge of contributing my stories to our ZOOM discussion this afternoon when something stopped me. Of course, the difficult years are long behind me, and I am usually at peace with my children's continuing sagas. But it does feel to me that contributing my story now and in this climate is defensive and dishonors the stories of the people at the heart of today's struggle. What would happen if I simply listened, then said, "I am sorry. I am so, so sorry."

May, 2020

ONCE A CATHOLIC, ALWAYS…?

It may be that all writers have produced passages, chapters, perhaps even books that they wish they hadn't written. Purple prose goes out of style, and indiscretions sometimes return to haunt us. Still, it never occurred to me that something I wrote eight or ten years ago in a somewhat less than serious mood would reappear so frequently now that I have changed my mind. The humor of the situation is heightened by the fact that the article in question dealt with ecclesiology.

When I first came to Pilgrim Place, I joined a writing group whose members promised each other that they would produce an article a year. Subsequently, those articles and reflections from the larger group that gathered each month to discuss the pieces became an annual chapbook. As one of the few Catholics in the community, I was the subject of a fair amount of curiosity from my Protestant neighbors. So finally, I wrote and presented "Why I stay Catholic."

I feel strongly that the Church's emphasis on ritual and sacrament highlights the importance of sacramental moments in daily life beyond a church. For example, every culture marks in some way all kinds of births, initiations, commitment moments, apologies and reconciliations, and finally, death. But I also lifted up some of the more whimsical saints who populate our calendar and our mythology with their feasts throughout the year. Protestants don't know about St. Christina the Astonishing, and I don't know how they would handle something like the pope's summarily removing St. Christopher from the church calendar several years ago. We Catholics took it in stride and kept our St. Christopher medals in our cars.

But last Advent, the news was full of idiotic shenanigans and dangerous pronouncements by various bishops and cardinals advising their flocks against Covid vaccination. Ultraconservative wealthy brethren locked arms with dissident clergy and political figures to mount an attack on the current Pontiff. I had had enough, and in the climate of attack and defense, I remembered my own struggles as an educated (Master in religious education, doctorate in ministry) woman in professional religious/spiritual service. I quit!

Son of a gun! Nary a day goes by without a notification from companies who keep track of professional writing to the effect that yet another scholar has searched for or cited that darned article. I barely resist the temptation to counter with another whimsical piece, "Why I got the hell out of Dodge." I play with the possible results. Would the scholar in Egypt who read my first piece now read the second and join me? Would The Index, the Church's former equivalent of the banned books bibliography, be revived just for me?

It's too easy to poke fun at all the troubles of the contemporary Catholic Church. I resist the currently popular category "spiritual but not religious," but here I am. Perhaps the virus and the resulting cancellation of church attendance everywhere allowed me to wonder how and if the Mass fit my own authentic spirituality. The truth is, it didn't fit. In a parish of 5000 families, I was invisible. I experienced God's presence in the kindliness among our small group who provided music when Saturday night Mass resumed. But when I could no longer drive at night, I knew that I would disappear in the crowd once more. In my mind, I could not handle being invisible before God.

I have had no regrets or second thoughts, and that seems odd for a cradle Catholic. I have not been idle, however. My sense of God's presence in the world, in the people around me, has remained and flourished. It's rather lovely not cringing daily when a priest somewhere tells his flock that God requires them to vote Republican, or when a cardinal piously declares that vaccinations contain microchips that allow the government to track its citizens.

"THIS PLACE IS NOT LONG FOR THE WORLD." – CHRISTIAN HYMN

It seems incongruous to think about this idea on this sunny afternoon in early October. Covid and the long days of isolation gave me time and perspective to think about what I really believe. I jettisoned Catholicism. No, that sounds as though it was rather sudden when in reality, I discovered that my spirituality had been shifting for years. As I aged, Augustine's and Ignatius' voices were replaced by the hymns of Sts. Francis and Hildegard. I found that life outside my window spoke to me more meaningfully than dialogues about good and evil and processes of discernment. Retirement gave me more time for reflection as my work became more solitary, less full of meetings and human in-person interaction, more time at my desk in front of my window.

"This train is bound for glory, this train. Don't carry nothing but the righteous and the holy, this train." (Woody Guthrie)

Still, "not long for the world," immediately became cloaked for me in images of clouds, angels, heaven and hell, judgment, purgatory, reward and punishment. I wonder if human beings are hard-wired that way. This morning, a Buddhist – Southern Baptist friend sent a reminiscence about an international panel of Buddhist and Christian scholars convened to discuss the origins of sin and evil. The Christian delegations presented Augustine's concept of original sin, while the Buddhists presented the notion of karma. Because the Westerners disagreed that life is only suffering, they also could not accept the notion of endless cycles of rebirth. For them, salvation by grace is accomplished in one lifetime alone.

"This world is dear to me/but heaven is my home. This is where I long to be/but heaven is my home." (Randy Newman)

Somehow, we immediately attach "salvation by grace" to good works. We may believe with Teilhard de Chardin that we are lifted by God, held back only by our anxiety about God's goodness and forgiveness. Like ducks, we float trustingly on the surface of the theological pond, but underneath, our feet are paddling with good works as fast as we can. Perhaps that is the actual original sin. But the dialogue continues nonetheless.

"Heaven lies about us in our infancy." (William Wordsworth. "Intimations of immortality")

"Not only about our infancy/Doth heaven with all its splendors lie;/Daily, with souls that cringe and plot,/ We Sinais climb and know it not." (James Russell Lowell. "The vision of Sir Launfal.")

Some months ago, I had the time and inclination to write about my operative theology. God knows I'm trying as hard as possible to be virtuous, and God also forgives me when I don't try. I believe God resides in me from the moment God blew the breath of life into Eve – - and Adam. These days, however, God treasures my joy at the pleasure of my student over newly discovered vocabulary words. I playfully reason that God needs a laugh today when a good joke makes its way through the lunch line outside our dining room. God takes pleasure in my wonder around my grandchildren's growing maturity, and God learns about irritation when I think they should be writing thank-you notes for Christmas gifts. As I join my daily contemplative prayer group, God teaches me that it is enough simply to rest. As I gradually float free from tangled creeds and church-centered rituals, I begin to suspect that all of our beliefs and denominations are myths. People since the creation have built stories to explain what is essentially a mystery: who are we, how did we get here, and what more? I watched the recent launches into space and wondered how other beings explain their existence. I read Native American stories, Buddhist myths, and Aztec sagas and conclude that any story I tell myself about God's relation to and with me is nothing more than my anxiety about my finiteness. For myself, any image I have about God is only my attempt to comfort myself in the face of the Unfathomable, the Absolute, the unlimited action of Love. It is enough now to rest in my old age.

MY PLACES

The only place I never put down roots was in my hometown, Lima, Ohio. It took a lifetime to wash the stain of that place from my heart. After that, I put down roots everywhere I've lived. In Columbus, Ohio, I blossomed in my work at Children's Hospital. In Jackson, Mississippi, I resonated with the sadness of the War of Northern Aggression, if not with its politics. Still, I delighted in Southern writers Flannery O'Connor, Eudora Welty, and Will Campbell. At Parkland Hospital in Dallas, Texas, I learned how to use power to ensure humane care for the indigent from birth to death. In North Carolina, I found a writerly home with Doris Betts, Clyde Edgerton, Lee Smith and Allan Gurganus, and I found my voice with physician friends and fellow researchers. My son and I discovered Dollar-a-Car Night at the Starlight Drive-In, and I was given my "real" name, Maggie, during 18 summers at bagpipe camp in Valle Crucis.

But it was in New York City that I rediscovered my gift for wonder, and found a mama as well. I had been recruited for a position at Sloan-Kettering Cancer Hospital as clinical pastoral educator, working with five chaplain residents and the department of psychiatry, and giving spiritual care to outpatients. My son was in a therapeutic group home in Wilmington and then in various adolescent psychiatry hospitals in New York. In a true miracle, I walked into a first-floor rent-stabilized apartment in an aging five-story brownstone walk-up half a block from Gracie mansion and the East River promenade. To this day, it is the only block in the city with birdhouses in each carefully tended tree. After the movers departed, leaving my earthly belongings out on the street, I staggered out to forage for dinner for my son and myself. Six blocks from home, I ran into an elderly wheelchair-bound woman. She called me over: "I hear you pray with folks." How did she know, and why, I wondered. "Would you pray with me," she asked. "I have a touch of bone cancer." Indeed! A touch? So the two of us had prayer right there, in the middle of an intersection. That was Nana, the 93-year-old Everybody's Grandma and Home Shopping Network maven.

Everyone on E. 83rd St. spent virtually every waking hour outside on our stoops. Honey Girl was my age, about 5 feet short and around 160 pounds. She had short pincurled bottle blonde hair and a vocabulary that would make a dockworker blush. Honey Girl's sons were city cops, and she put that leverage to good use when she obtained a bootleg key for the fire hydrant out front. We had monthly block meetings, and street parties on every holiday and many weekends. Folks may still be talking about the annual street fair the year the featured entertainers were a 60-year-old paunchy Elvis impersonator and my pipe band, performing together as the day wore on and the beer got warm.

On Christmas, we went caroling by candlelight with hot cocoa brewed over somebody's hibachi. Big John and Big Mary were an enormous couple who spent every night together on one stoop, each listening to his/her own transistor radio. Honey Girl decided they should get married, and when Christmas passed without a diamond engagement ring on Mary's finger, it was said that Honey Girl bought one and proposed in John's stead. After one blizzard, they built anatomically correct snowmen atop each car on the street.

My son adored Honey Girl, and I relaxed into the care of a wise, generous mama for the first time in my life. I think Honey Girl had always wished for a daughter, and I was grateful that she found one. At my installation, the Rockefellers provided a lavish, catered, and eye-popping buffet before the service at the gothic Episcopal church near East 60th. I brought Honey Girl and Veasna as my family. I could tell that, certainly for the first time in her life, Honey Girl was impressed. Walking home afterward, she commented, "Margot, that was a <u>very</u> nice spread. Only one thing was lacking." "What was that, Honey Girl?" I asked. "Velveeta cheese!" she replied.

Sure enough, when I arrived home after work the next afternoon, she called over from her stoop next door, "Come here! Take a load off." She patted the step for me to sit next to her. Reaching behind her, she pulled from her grocery bag the largest jar of Velveeta cheese I had ever seen, a family-sized box of Ritz crackers, and a butter knife. With Rockefellian formality, she gravely slathered cheese on a cracker, and offered it to me. I took a bite. "See! Velveeta cheese! <u>That's</u> what was missing!" she said. And she was right.

I have always been adventurous and fearless, often because I had no choice. But I absolutely nestled into Manhattan. I did my grocery shopping in Chinatown, where I stuck out as the only tall white woman purchasing 50 pounds of rice and 5 pounds of fresh ginger at a time. Street vendors quickly learned my favorite kind of noodle and how much I loved trading photos of kids and grandkids, no words needed.

Each month, I spent one Sunday at the Cloisters, where I nested on a stone bench right in front of the heat vent in winter and the AC in summer, while I prayed, thought and wrote. I found a $12 ticket to the opening night of a Candide revival on Broadway, where I discovered first, that my seat was on the stage, and second, that I loved doing over-the-top curtain calls with the "real" cast. I spent all night at the Cathedral of St. John the Divine to watch the sun come up through the rose window at each solstice and to get an aisle seat for the procession of the animals on St. Francis's feast. I loved playing with my band down Fifth Avenue for the 10,000 Pipers Festival. I was proud when we helped a start-up band, the nation's only gay-lesbian-Harley-motorcycle-club pipe band, gain a following with the heretofore bigoted local firefighters.

Whenever I returned to Manhattan from a far-off conference or meeting, I could tell I was home because the city felt like popcorn. Six weeks after the Twin Towers fell, I was invited to Norway to teach for several weeks. On returning that time, I was overcome by the heaviness, the palpable grief of the city. I lasted for another year before my spirit and the city felt unbearably broken, and I fled to work with rural pastors across the Midwest. I have heard that the city never really recovered.

July, 2020

LOSE A PLACE; FIND A PLACE

"Maggie, I received your deposit for our tour of four African countries, and I'm afraid we can't accept your application. We had some complaints that you held back the other folks on the Central Asia tour, and I have to look out for their interests and your protection."

Several months earlier, I had gone on a trip of a lifetime. I signed on with a company specializing in low-cost expeditions for teachers. After three years of planning, I found myself in a group of special needs-to-community college level teachers for a month-long tour of the four countries on the Silk Road in Central Asia. For better or for worse, I went into the experience with my customary enthusiasm for new adventures. I should have known better. Within the first several days, I realized that no matter what I did or said, this was not going to be a warm, fuzzy group. When one of the teachers introduced himself as an art instructor, I asked what medium he worked in. "I don't!" he barked, his last words to me for the rest of the trip. It was impossible to carry on a conversation of more than two words at a time before the ubiquitous cell phones intervened. At the same time, I discovered that I was being hazed, when I was approached by two of the women. What could I reply to challenges like, "What's with the black knee socks?" and "Why do you wear your hair all frizzy?" besides, "I have to wear support stockings," and "It grows that way."

I seldom cry anymore. At 81, I've seen many situations worse to cry about than the tour company manager's call. Nevertheless, I sat in the car with my cell phone, and wept. At first, I was ashamed, as though I hadn't measured up, performed well enough, been unlikable or lazy. Then I was angry. Did I delay the others when I had my suitcase at the bus by 6:00 AM each morning for 8 o'clock departures… when the rest of the group gathered at 8:45? Who was it who canceled group supper reservations at fine ethnic restaurants because they insisted on American-style pizza and Starbucks coffee—in Uzbekistan?

The tour company manager attempted to mollify me. Almost certainly afraid that I would turn my anger on him, he quickly crooned, "It's hard to admit you're old. Why, I'm only 44, and I can't play handball the way I used to." I'm glad I didn't respond—at least I think I didn't—with the first words that came to my mind: "Go to hell!"

Then, as my anger and shame subsided, I became aware of another feeling, one worth much more in exploring than four weeks with a gaggle of bored and disillusioned schoolteachers. I remembered recently writing somewhat blithely about letting go through the years of my beloved Vespa GT, then my custom-made bagpipes with the beautiful silverwork, then my painting, my needlework, my handwriting. No, this was different. Sitting in the car, I envisioned the future me, perhaps blind, probably dependent on others to serve my meals, cut my food, brush my hair, choose my clothing. Now, I can drive myself to the grocery twice in one day if I have forgotten something. Now, I can join the early morning walkers at the local mall if I wish, without having to find someone to drive me there. Now, I can cook a meal for my friends; who does that for the dwellers in Assisted Living? What else will I lose, and when?

    I have been independent all my life. Now I live in a continuing care retirement community (CCRC) with a long history of friendships throughout so that we seem comfortable with frailty and mortality, both others' and ours. I learned this morning that I may not be so comfortable after all. I may choose to use a cane or walker in our dining room, but I fear and perhaps would resent being required to do so by someone else. Staring up close at the limitations pronounced by the unwitting tour company manager, I have to look at limitations pronounced both by others and by my own body…without consulting with me first. It doesn't seem fair, but it is life, isn't it?

September 1, 2022

PRENDS COURAGE!

Although I had visited New York City as a teen, I thought I had met my match when I later moved there. Still, the process was eased by a cascade of minor—and major—miracles. While my time, money, and the list of available apartments were all short, I managed to walk into an opening on a block straight out of "A Tree Grows In Brooklyn." Flanked by Gracie Mansion and multimillion-dollar high-rises, our one block of rent-controlled five-story brownstone walk-ups was home to the city's most colorful cast of characters. Tightknit, everybody knew and cared about everybody's business. Our anchors were Honey Girl on one end and Crazy Louise on the other. Louise lived on the sidewalk because her apartment was crammed to the door with stuff salvaged from the block's dumpsters. She was French-Canadian, orphaned as a child, and had a heart of gold and a voice like a foghorn. My son, a Cambodian war survivor, was a handful, spending most of his time in local psychiatric hospitals for PTSD. Louise could always tell when he and I were having a bad day, week, or month. She would move over on her stoop, patting the step for me to sit down beside her. I would pour out my sorrow, and Louise would listen. "Take courage," was her benediction. And then, lifting her 80-year-old thin bones to her feet, she would raise her fist and shout, "Prends courage!!" Lowering her voice, she would whisper, "That means, 'Take courage,' but what the hell does that mean? Now, 'Prends courage!' That says it all!" That really does "say it all," when nothing at all can be said.

Now, "Courage" has my parents' faces. They had a glamorous life in depression era theatre before the arrival of children called them to settle down in the much less glamorous setting of small-town Ohio. The world was different then. Young people today are freer to think in terms of what they'd <u>like</u> to do with their lives or even to put off such decisions until the way seems clear. My grandmother was widowed about the time I was born, and my father's duty was to care for her and his growing family. They started a family business of stage scenery, lighting, and sound, but what put food on the table most reliably was dad's second shift as a projectionist in the local theater. I asked him once just before he died what his work life had been like all those years. "Well, it was exciting to have a hand in developing the talkies and Cinemascope, but the last few years, it was just loading reels into the projector, nothing creative like the old days." I admire their ability to find meaning in their work as long and as well as they could, and to care for us, too. Their courage helped them to create a home for us all, even on those days when that must have seemed pure drudgery.

Courage? I think of a group of inmates in rural Missouri prisons. My tiny inner-city, predominantly African-American Catholic church decorated the sanctuary with three large banners listing the names of "Our members in college," "Our members in the military," and "Our members in prison." Fifteen or so years ago, I took on the ministry of writing to those on the third banner. In some ways, we have become family to one another. Velma sent me a paper flower she had been allowed to make in a craft class once before the new warden canceled all such activities. She mused that at 30, she had spent over half of her life in prison, and she was terrified as her release date came nearer. I rejoiced with David when he got to exercise outside for one hour each day after many years in "The Hole." Willie shared his poetry but despaired of ever getting his GED. Courage for these men and women means total subjugation to a racist system that aims to punish in every way possible, with no pretense of rehabilitation. Their courage allows them to deal with dehumanizing injustice, guilt, and shame and be open to small glimmers of joy and hope.

I suspect that most of us can look back on days, perhaps even years, when there was little to keep us going except the promises we've made. Courage is the virtue that gets us out of bed every morning, opens our hearts to moments of grace, and leads us to eventually proclaim with Jacob (Genesis 28:16), "Truly, the Lord is in this place, although I did not know it." Until then, "Prends courage!"

February, 2022

IF I COULD JUST LISTEN...

Like a growing number of elders these days, I have chosen to live in a retirement community. We are an active community. Members have vocationally or avocationally dedicated their lives and resources to social justice and the environment as a condition of admittance, and once here, that commitment continues. In addition, everyone works to the limits of their energy, time, and resources to keep the community solvent and even to provide for those households who cannot afford living expenses.

On the face of it, this is indeed laudable. We have an oversized voice at the town Council, advocating for low-cost housing, the homeless, and elder services. We are often referred to as "the conscience of Claremont," although the income and racial differences between the high North end and the low South end of town reveal that there is more work to do.

But something happened to me the other day that has given me pause. I decided to take a walk around the campus last Sunday morning. Several blocks from home, I tripped on an uneven sidewalk, scraping my chin, nose, and eyeglasses, badly tearing my hand, and leaving me with a three-day concussion headache. With no one in sight, I limped back to the clinic on campus, where the weekend nurse mopped the blood off my clothing and bandaged my hand and arm. I trudged home, leaking self-pity on the way. During the following days, I maintained my meeting schedule with clients and students. However, my anger mounted with each passing day as neighbors waited for me to open doors and emailed requests and reminders to drive them to doctors' appointments and other tasks. When my writers' group shared my self-righteous rage, I got enough distance to be able to laugh at myself, which is always salvific for me. Over time, however, I am reminded of a perspective I invariably lose when I am in need.

There are mixed messages on all sides here, more than enough to go around. Sometimes I wonder if my wish to be cared for is so palpable that it drives people away. On the other hand, people here often describe me as "kind," which I am beginning to hear as the assumption that I will always and universally be of unilateral service to them. I spent my career in a "service" industry, where I learned to be observant of people's needs, both evident and unspoken. While I know that pastoring and administrative positions were not without their challenges, few pastors opened their own doors or brought a covered dish to parish suppers. I recall my New York pipe teacher's invitation to play at the Irish Arts Center ceildh and pot luck dinner. Because I rode on the subway, I could not manage both pipes and casserole. When I arrived sans pipes, I explained that to my teacher. "What do you mean!" he roared. "<u>You</u> are <u>The Piper</u>! The Piper <u>never</u> brings a dish. You bring your <u>pipes</u>." Same for the pastor, the priest, the dean, the chairman, the president, and perhaps for most males in authority.

My second learning is that for better or for worse, and usually for worse, we are all old here. This one is harder for me to come to terms with. None of us are getting out of here alive. Covid hasn't changed any of us, but it has forced many of us to flee to the surface of our relationships, where there is no air for more than our own wants. It has been more than a year and a half since we've been able to resume our community meal together. Many of our connection times—noon meal, memorial services, weekly Vespers, Sunday services that we provide for the homebound — have disappeared. It's hard to remember who among the fragile among us have died during this time. Twenty-four have left us, and we were not allowed to bless them on their way.

And the still living? We are so chained to our self-absorption that there's not enough energy or attention left to notice who can't fetch their lunchbox at noon. I struggle every day to put a floppy cardboard carton full of wet food into my basket along with containers of fruit, salad, bread, milk, salad dressing and dessert. Every day the old ones behind me wonder loudly and petulantly who's holding up the line. The young server sees my struggle and, without fuss or nudging, comes around the counter to gently steady my elbow.

So as I write to unravel my feelings about my accident and the community's inability to respond to me, I grieve more than my untrustworthy gait. And I'm angry about more than my neighbors' insensitivity to me. There must be times when I am equally insensitive and unobservant. Those will probably come more and more frequently as I continue to age. I am comforted and reassured by being known as "kind" now, and I wonder if I will lose that as I become more fragile. Will I become less able to keep my cranky, irascible side under wraps? And what will happen to me when I can no longer earn my keep by being nice?

HEIRLOOM

One of the classic understatements in our family's lore revolved around the relationship between my mother and her mother-in-law, my father's mother. They did not get along! Portraits of my grandmother show a proud, dignified Victorian matron with her children at her knee and her husband by her side. Granted, that was soon to change, as her husband died in an industrial accident. My uncle ran away from home, and my aunt followed, leaving my father to provide for her. She treated my mother like a country bumpkin. That did not sit well with my mother, who had a college degree in music performance, and was a gifted pianist. As the eldest grandchild, I became the surrogate of both in their very civilized, under-the-table war. The ammunition for some of those skirmishes was a set of silverware.

What she lacked in education, my grandmother made up in dinner-table cutlery. With three small children and a husband in poor health, my mother kept the family business going and all of us fed and clothed. Silverware was the least of her worries, although I suspect that my grandmother's patrician attitude rankled.

When my grandmother died, the silverware came to us. By the time I understood its symbolism, many pieces were missing or scratched and worn. Many years later, when I left the convent with nothing to my name, my mother gave me what was left of the set. I suspect she was glad to have it out of the house. Out of a sense of loyalty to my mother, I continued the mistreatment of the silverware. One teaspoon handle bore scars inflicted by the garbage disposer.

As time went on, however, I gained a tad of wisdom about the family dynamic, the silverware, and my role in the whole thing. One day at a craft fair, I came upon an eccentric silversmith. Wearing a Cossack costume, he had set up his workbench and blowtorch and was merrily turning all manner of silver serving dishes into marvelous mythic creatures. Soup terrines became genial dinosaurs with sugar bowl heads and serving spoon legs. Teapots gained personalities.

Inspired, I remembered that set in the silverware drawer in my kitchen at home. I ran home, wrapped the entire set in a dishtowel, and returned with a wish list in my hand. Several months later, I received a large box filled with small cotton drawstring bags. There were key fobs for my sisters' husbands. My daughter and I each had teaspoon rings, mine with a garbage disposer scar for memory's sake. The small teaspoons became earrings, and the hollow knife handles became beautiful stickpin bud vases for a lapel. Everyone loved the jewelry. But the thing that made me happiest was Grandmother. I don't think it's just my imagination that she rests easier now, and perhaps she and my mother have made peace.

Years later, when I moved to New York City, I quickly learned that discarded household goods never made it to the trash containers at the curbs. On our block, Saturday was Good Trash Day. Folks drove in from near and far to see what was available. One could—and often did—furnish one's apartment wall to wall by Saturday night. Manhattanites usually knew each neighborhood's trash day, and planned accordingly.

So it was that one day as I was hurrying to work, I had to step over furniture and small appliances that someone, perhaps adult children of a deceased mom or dad, hurriedly threw away. I wouldn't have given it a second thought until I saw almost underfoot the remains of a well-used set of silverware. I continued for several steps but then turned back. Stooping, I hitched my skirt above my knees and scooped the pieces into my briefcase.

Winter is not leaving easily now, and it's dark and cold even on a Southern California evening. I think I will heat some soup for supper, and I shall serve it in my favorite handmade soup bowl. And best of all, I shall sip from a well-used, scarred silver soup spoon, while my mother and grandmother… and another woman, nameless… look on with satisfaction.

November, 2021

TRANSCENDENCE VS FEAR/ FOLLY

Onlookers might not know this about me, but I have a fairly active compliant streak in my being, as befits the eldest daughter in a 1950s vintage Catholic family. We didn't look at all like the TV commercial families, but God knows we tried. So when Erickson speaks about elders and living into transcendence, God knows I will try to do that as well.

According to Erikson, transcendence is an older person's moving beyond concerns about body image and physical limitation, social isolation and past regrets to an acceptance and appreciation of limitations, solitude, and peace as one grows closer to death. These themes are emphasized in the later theory of gerotranscendence, developed to give caregivers an understanding of the "old old."

However, my County Tyrone forebears on one side and the Norman Scots on the other side won't let me go into the "gentle night" ("Do not go gentle into that good night," Dylan Thomas) of that kind of transcendence quite so easily, or perhaps not at all. To be fair, perhaps I haven't given Erickson a fair chance. God knows, I would love to have a sense of proportion about my world, as though my upraised arm were not the only thing that keeps the stars in their orbit or my children from losing their battles against a challenging and intolerant world. (Exodus 17:9-13) But my "day labor" is not yet totally denied light ("On His Blindness," John Milton), and there is much to rage against on this earth. As I sit down to write, NPR is broadcasting a program on the devastated and foreshortened life that Haiti sugarcane workers lead to keep sugar in my food. I wonder how I could help them. I keep flying after one cause after another against the day when I will be completely unable to minister in any way at all. If non-transcendence is wondering whether God and the world will get along without me, that's an embarrassing piece of me these days, with so much need everywhere I turn.

But there really is more. My roots are in this world, right now, today, rather than in the cool calm of solitary contemplation of my death. My focus these days is on the crowded birdfeeder on my patio … in the odd-looking but delicious orange–sized yellow eggplant fruits that now drip from the dying seedling I rescued from the 99 Cent store… in the pleasure my Alzheimer's neighbors and their "minders" take from the splashing in the birdbath outside my window. The 125 fruit trees nurtured for the 110 years of Pilgrim Place are heavy with fruit this season, and we have enthusiastically added a new goal for the money we pruners will raise with the proceeds; economic diversity for this "white bread" community. I can't let go of my sense of responsibility for the trees and the people, and my joy that my neighbors who have worked so hard for justice need worry no longer at the end of their lives.

One of my earliest memories is of my mother sitting in an old rocking chair reading to us from our favorite children's book, "The littlest Angel." Now no doubt in some circles theologically passé, that unfolded my atlas of places where God appears and things that God cares about. Still, every once in a while, I look over my shoulder and wonder if I'm doing "it" right. The other day, I took to my peer review partner my fear that a client and I weren't being serious enough, that we laugh so much. He wisely observed, "That's how God gets to laugh, when you do."

No, I cannot bear to "transcend." God gets to worry about my children when I do, and it's God's chance to marvel at the dimensions of the nearby mountains, because I do. How would God know the warmth of Phoebe on my lap if not for me? Who will mourn the 35-year-old, imprisoned for more than half her life, who died before she learned to read, her only wish. Who will tell her story? I do want to have a sense of proportion, a long view. But I am angry about that injustice. I want the "I live on Tongva land" sign on my fence to mean something now!

Fifteen years or so ago, I joined a tour group on the climb to the top of Mount Sinai. All night I toiled with many hundreds of other pilgrims in total darkness up perilous foot-high steps. An hour before dawn, I could go no further, so I crawled to a sharp precipice overlooking hundreds of miles of solitary desert. At first, I was heartbroken, having feared that, like Moses, I was unworthy to reach the "promised land" at the top. But as I lay watching the mountains in the far distance, first dawn, and then sunrise broke over the entire expanse of that wilderness. I remembered Teilhard de Chardin's Mass Over the Universe: "Over every living thing which is to spring up, to grow, to flower, to ripen during this day, I say again the words: <u>this</u> is my body, and over every death force which waits in readiness to corrode, to wither, to cut down, speak again Your commanding words which express the supreme mystery of faith: <u>this</u> is my blood."

Pierre Teilhard de Chardin: Hymn of the Universe: "Over there, on the horizon, the sun has just touched with light the outermost fringe of the eastern sky. Once again, beneath this moving sheet of fire, the living surface of the earth wakes and trembles, and once again begins its fearful travail. I will place on my paten, O God, the harvest to be won by this renewal of labor. Into my chalice I shall pour all the sap which is to be pressed out this day from the Earth's fruits."

October 8, 2020

ABOUT THE AUTHOR

Margot Hover, D.Min. ACPE/NACC Supervisor Emerita spent her pre-retirement career first as high school English and drama teacher, then as teaching chaplain at Dallas Parkland Hospital, Duke University, Sloan Kettering Cancer Center, and finally, working with pastors throughout rural Illinois and Missouri. She was foster parent for troubled teens before adopting two Cambodian refugee children, and is now proud grandmother of five. She currently ministers as a Spiritual Director. She lives at Pilgrim Place, a retirement community working for peace, justice, and care of the environment.

112 N. Harvard Ave. #65
Claremont, CA 91711

chapbooks@bamboodartpress.com

www.bamboodartpress.com

CPSIA information can be obtained
at www.ICGtesting.com
Printed in the USA
LVHW051937070423
743801LV00007B/107